To the "Gator Man" —
Always Remember your trip —

Sincerely
Mindy Taylor Stokes
Apr. 02

GASTON
the
Green-Nosed
Alligator

GASTON
the
Green-Nosed
Alligator

Written and Illustrated by James Rice

Full-color Edition

PELICAN PUBLISHING COMPANY

Gretna 1999

First edition, September 1974
Second printing, September 1976
Third printing, September 1982
Fourth printing, September 1989
Fifth printing, September 1994
Second edition, September 1999

The word "Pelican" and the depiction of a pelican are trademarks of Pelican Publishing Company, Inc., and are registered in the U.S. Patent and Trademark Office.

Library of Congress Cataloging-in-Publication Data

Rice, James, 1934-
    Gaston the green-nosed alligator / written and illustrated by James Rice.
       p.   c.m.
    Summary: Santa Claus moves his headquarters to the Louisiana bayou
and replaces his reindeer with flying alligators.
    ISBN 1-56554-285-1 (alk. paper)
    1. Santa Claus Juvenile fiction.   [1. Santa Claus Fiction.
2. Christmas Fiction. 3. Alligators Fiction. 4. Stories in rhyme.]
I. Title.
PZ8.3.R36Gas 1999
[E]--dc21
                                                  99-31229
                                                    CIP

Printed in Korea

Published by Pelican Publishing Company, Inc.
1000 Burmaster Street, Gretna, Louisiana 70053

GASTON
THE GREEN-NOSED ALLIGATOR

Quaint ol' Santa
    in his house made of ice,
Was working as hard
    as a barn full of mice.

Ol' Santa seemed worried,
    his face didn't glow.
The reindeer were shirking
    and working too slow.

Their reasons were many,
    their excuses were old—
Prancer sprained his ankle,
    and Donner caught a cold.

Vixen picked up a splinter,
    and Dasher split his hoof,
They'd all crash-landed
    on top of a roof.

And most tragic of all
    another problem arose,
The light had gone out
    on poor Rudolph's nose.

The reindeer were not all
    that gave Santa distress,
The whole North Pole business
    was now in a mess.

With ice on his whiskers,
    and frost on his breath,
An ol' man like Santa
    might shiver to death.

He searched the world over
   in less than a week,
To find the best spot
   to warm his cold feet.

In South Louisiana
   he found the right place,
With warm bayou waters
   and trees hung with lace.

The reindeer last Christmas
    had nearly run late,
Because of a rainstorm
    in this very state.

Snow was no problem
    they'd fly through with ease.
But that kind of storm
    almost leveled the trees.

Santa poled down the bayou
and let his thoughts roam.
The problem's solution
he'd find near his home.

From out of the corner
of his left eye he spied
In the treetops a sight
that all logic defied.

For there flew ol' Gaston
    as sure as you please,
Swooping and gliding
    through the tops of the trees.

"*Sacre!* Look at Gaston,
    something sure is not right.
He flies like a bird!
    Twice as fast! What a flight!"

While ol' Gaston flew
he put on a show,
The envy of the gators
he left down below.

"Stop, you strange creature,
and come here to me!"
Shouted ol' Santa,
exploding with glee.

His problem was solved,
no more reindeer he'd need.
Ol' Gaston would help,
there was no need to plead.

He'd train seven others
to fly with a skiff,
Full of toys and goodies
and every good gift.

But they'd crash into trees
    and fall on their tails,
They'd try it again
    and still they would fail.

But they wouldn't give up
    till they'd mastered the skill,
Of gliding through treetops
    with never a spill.

Now practice was over,
    it was near time to leave,
For in a few hours
    'twould be Christmas Eve.

They loaded the gift bags
    in the skiff up so high,
Then hitched up the gators
    and got ready to fly.

They didn't miss a stop
      on their fantastic flight,
New records for speed
      were the standard that night.

And back on the bayou
    at just before dawn,
A sleepy old Cajun
    looked up with a yawn,

To see in the shadows
    an impossible scene—
A little old man
    with an outlandish team.

And a voice saying clearly,
    before he vanished in tow,
"Merry Christmas to all,
    till I saw ya some mo!"